EASY AND FUN
KATAKANA

Basic Japanese Writing for Loanwords and Emphasis

Kiyomi Ogawa

Edited by Orrin Cummins

Stone Bridge Press • *Berkeley, California*

Preface

Some Japanese learners do not place a high importance on learning katakana characters. To be honest, even as a teacher of the language I didn't fully appreciate their value at first. But when I began to observe my surroundings with a more critical eye, I noticed the incredible number of katakana terms in use. It is not an exaggeration to say that practically every word on many restaurant and café menus is written in katakana.

Originally, katakana was used only for *gairaigo*—words imported into the language from other countries—but it is now heavily used in magazines and advertisements due to its inherent "cool factor." Since katakana is used mostly for nouns, understanding it can help you grasp the general idea of a sentence even if you can't fully decipher the grammar. And compared to kanji, katakana characters are much easier to write.

The issue that most foreigners have with katakana has to do with pronunciation. Although most katakana words have their origins in other languages, the way they are pronounced in Japanese is usually quite different. This is partly because the Japanese language is relatively flat, without much rising or falling intonation. So don't get discouraged if it takes you a few seconds to understand a freshly encountered katakana word! The problem is exacerbated by the sizable number of katakana words whose meanings have drifted away from those they held in their original languages.

In this book, I have included many illustrations so that you can know the meanings of words at a glance and get a visual sense of how katakana is used in everyday Japanese life. You will also become familiar with a number of popular *wasei-eigo* terms, some of which seem like English words but won't be recognized as such in English-speaking countries.

Mastering katakana will make reading Japanese more enjoyable!

Kiyomi Ogawa

カバーデザイン：岩目地英樹（コムデザイン）

まえがき

　日本語学習者のなかには、カタカナはひらがなや漢字ほど重要ではないと考えている人がいるようです。実は、私自身も教える立場としてあまり重要視していませんでした。しかし、あたりを見渡してみれば、カタカナ言葉の多いこと！　特にレストランやカフェのメニューはほとんど全部カタカナといっても過言ではありません。

　カタカナはもともと外来語だけのために使われていましたが、今ではかっこいいからという理由で、雑誌や広告などで多く使われています。さらに、ひらがなは助詞や動詞の一部であるのに対して、カタカナは名詞に使うため、カタカナが読めれば文法がわからなくても意味を理解することができるという利点もあります。書き方も漢字に比べればとてもシンプルで書きやすいでしょう。

　問題は、発音が本来のものとはかなり違って聞こえるということです。日本語はとても平たんな音で、上がり下がりがあまりありません。ですから、カタカナが読めても、一体何のことか理解するのに時間がかかるかもしれません。また元の英語の意味とは違った意味で使われることもありますので、注意しなければなりません。

　本書では、一目見てすぐに意味が分かるように、たくさんのイラストを使用し、カタカナがどんな風に日本の生活に使われているかを視覚的に学ぶことができるように工夫しました。また、日本人がよく使う和製英語も学ぶことができます。

　カタカナをマスターすれば、色々な物を読むのが楽しくなりますよ！

小川清美

How to Use this Book

First, learn how to read and write katakana by working your way through chapter 2.

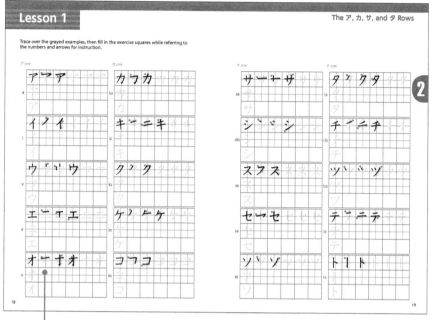

—— Trace and write the characters using the correct stroke order.

Chapter 3 focuses on how katakana words are used in everyday Japanese life.

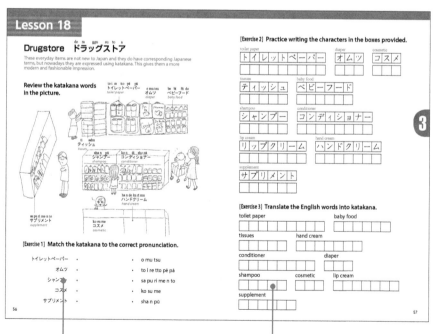

—— Complete the reading and writing exercises in each lesson.

In chapter 4 you can build your reading skills while learning katakana terms related to people, countries, and business.

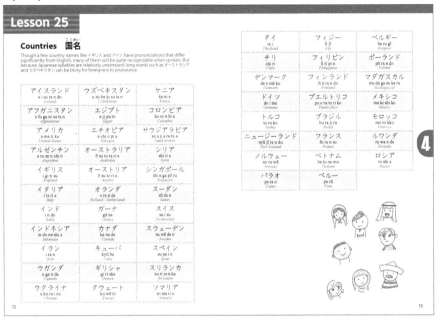

Finally, chapter 5 introduces *wasei-eigo* terms. These are very useful for understanding native Japanese speakers.

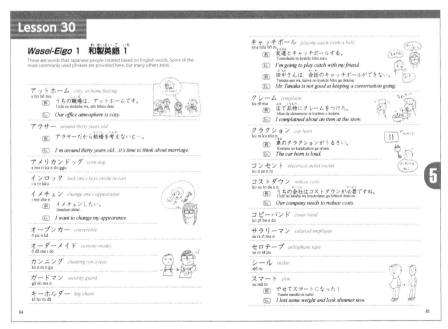

Even if you don't have time to complete the writing exercises, I recommend that you at least read chapters 2 and 3 since they contain many indispensable terms for conversing in Japanese.

CONTENTS

Chapter 4 People, Places, and Business 71
第4章　人・場所・ビジネスに関するカタカナ

Chapter 5 *Wasei-Eigo* and Other Terms 83
第5章　和製英語など

Chapter 1

History and Usage

第 1 章　カタカナの歴史と使われ方

History of Katakana

It is said that katakana was originally developed around the eighth century for reading Buddhist sutras transmitted from China. To aid in reciting the texts, monks created a sort of shorthand by simplifying the Chinese characters. Other theories exist, but this is the most generally accepted one.

In contrast to hiragana characters, each of which represents a simplified version of an entire kanji, the katakana characters were created by taking only a portion of the corresponding kanji.

Kanji		Katakana	Kanji		Hiragana
伊	→	イ	以	→	い
呂	→	ロ	呂	→	ろ

The monks added these modified characters next to the kanji as a pronunciation guide. Although the katakana script started out as a simple note-taking method for Buddhist monks and intellectuals, starting in the Meiji era it gained popularity among common citizens as a way to express foreign words (*gairaigo*). During this period, women even used katakana to write their names.

Katakana is currently taught after hiragana at elementary schools in Japan.

カタカナの歴史

カタカナは8世紀ごろ中国から仏教が伝わった時に、仏教の経典を書き写すために作られたと言われています。僧侶たちが漢字の一部を簡素化したのです。他の説もありますが、これがいまのところ有力なようです。

ひらがなは漢字全体を簡素化していますが、カタカナは漢字の一部だけを取って簡素化しています。

漢字		カタカナ	漢字		ひらがな
伊	→	イ	以	→	い
呂	→	ロ	呂	→	ろ

このように簡単にしたものを僧侶たちは漢字の横につけて読んでいました。ですから、もともとは僧侶や知識人が漢字を読む際の注記として使っていましたが、明治以降に外来語に使われるようになり、一般の人々にも使われるようになったようです。またその頃、女性の名前にも多く使われました。

現在は小学校でひらがなの次に学ばれています。

Using Katakana

Katakana is used for *gairago*, or words from other languages which have been adopted into Japanese. This of course includes the names of foreign countries and people, but also a great many other terms related to food, technology, and miscellaneous products. Although katakana words are based on these foreign counterparts, their pronunciations can differ significantly from the original words, making them surprisingly tricky for foreigners.

And even in cases where a Japanese word already exists for a particular concept, *gairaigo* is often used in magazines and advertisements because it sounds stylish to Japanese people. Among these are a number of words whose meanings or usages differ from those found in the source languages. Such terms are known as *wasei-eigo*, or "Japanese English."

The katakana script also has a certain stylistic effect from a visual standpoint. Compared to hiragana or kanji, katakana creates a casual or comical impression; this is why colloquial expressions and onomatopoeia are often written in katakana. Katakana is widely used for company and product names for the same reason.

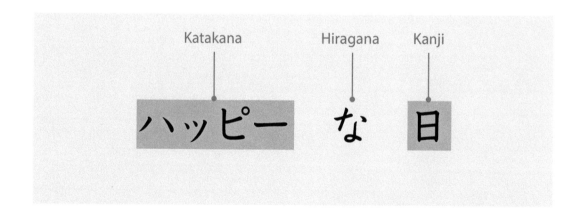

Katakana	Hiragana	Kanji
ハッピー	な	日

カタカナの使われ方

カタカナは主に外来語つまり外国から来た言葉に使います。国の名前や人名をはじめ、食べ物、雑貨、IT 用語などに多く使われています。しかし、発音は本来の外国語とはかなり違って聞こえるので外国人には難しいようです。

また、外来語で本来の日本語表記がある場合でも、外国語のほうが日本人にはおしゃれに聞こえるので、雑誌や広告ではカタカナを用いることが多いようです。中には外国語の本来の意味から外れている言葉もあり、それらを和製英語と呼んでいます。

カタカナには視覚的な効果もあります。ひらがなや漢字と比べて、カタカナは軽くておもしろい印象があるので、くだけた表現やオノマトペをカタカナで表すことが多くあります。同様の理由で会社名や商品名にも使用されています。

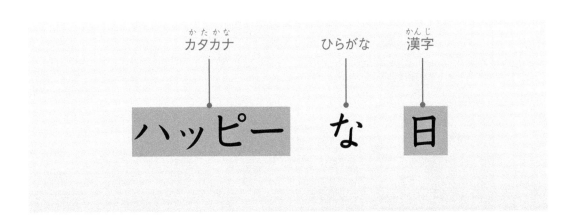

カタカナ　　　ひらがな　　　漢字

ハッピー　な　日

Characters and Pronunciation

This syllable set is primarily used for words borrowed from other languages, but it is also widely adopted into logos, slang speech, and other formats.

Katakana

Basic syllables

a	ア	i	イ	u	ウ	e	エ	o	オ
ka	カ	ki	キ	ku	ク	ke	ケ	ko	コ
sa	サ	shi	シ	su	ス	se	セ	so	ソ
ta	タ	chi	チ	tsu	ツ	te	テ	to	ト
na	ナ	ni	ニ	nu	ヌ	ne	ネ	no	ノ
ha/wa	ハ	hi	ヒ	fu	フ	he/e	ヘ	ho	ホ
ma	マ	mi	ミ	mu	ム	me	メ	mo	モ
ya	ヤ			yu	ユ			yo	ヨ
ra	ラ	ri	リ	ru	ル	re	レ	ro	ロ
wa	ワ							wo/o	ヲ
n	ン								

kya	キャ	kyu	キュ	kyo	キョ
sha	シャ	shu	シュ	sho	ショ
cha	チャ	chu	チュ	cho	チョ
nya	ニャ	nyu	ニュ	nyo	ニョ
hya	ヒャ	hyu	ヒュ	hyo	ヒョ
mya	ミャ	myu	ミュ	myo	ミョ

rya	リャ	ryu	リュ	ryo	リョ

Modified syllables

ga	ガ	gi	ギ	gu	グ	ge	ゲ	go	ゴ
za	ザ	ji	ジ	zu	ズ	ze	ゼ	zo	ゾ
da	ダ	ji	ヂ	zu	ヅ	de	デ	do	ド
ba	バ	bi	ビ	bu	ブ	be	ベ	bo	ボ
pa	パ	pi	ピ	pu	プ	pe	ペ	po	ポ

gya	ギャ	gyu	ギュ	gyo	ギョ
ja	ジャ	ju	ジュ	jo	ジョ

bya	ビャ	byu	ビュ	byo	ビョ
pya	ピャ	pyu	ピュ	pyo	ピョ

The hiragana syllabary contains 46 basic characters. Five of these represent syllables (あ, い, う, え, お) which are phonetically combined with consonants to form the remaining characters. In addition, many characters can be modified using the accent marks 「゙」 or 「゚」 to form slightly different sounds. Variants created by appending a small や, ゆ, or よ also exist.

Hiragana

Basic syllables

a	あ	i	い	u	う	e	え	o	お
ka	か	ki	き	ku	く	ke	け	ko	こ
sa	さ	shi	し	su	す	se	せ	so	そ
ta	た	chi	ち	tsu	つ	te	て	to	と
na	な	ni	に	nu	ぬ	ne	ね	no	の
ha/wa	は	hi	ひ	fu	ふ	he/e	へ	ho	ほ
ma	ま	mi	み	mu	む	me	め	mo	も
ya	や			yu	ゆ			yo	よ
ra	ら	ri	り	ru	る	re	れ	ro	ろ
wa	わ							wo/o	を
n	ん								

kya	きゃ	kyu	きゅ	kyo	きょ
sha	しゃ	shu	しゅ	sho	しょ
cha	ちゃ	chu	ちゅ	cho	ちょ
nya	にゃ	nyu	にゅ	nyo	にょ
hya	ひゃ	hyu	ひゅ	hyo	ひょ
mya	みゃ	myu	みゅ	myo	みょ

rya	りゃ	ryu	りゅ	ryo	りょ

Modified syllables

ga	が	gi	ぎ	gu	ぐ	ge	げ	go	ご
za	ざ	ji	じ	zu	ず	ze	ぜ	zo	ぞ
da	だ	ji	ぢ	zu	づ	de	で	do	ど
ba	ば	bi	び	bu	ぶ	be	べ	bo	ぼ
pa	ぱ	pi	ぴ	pu	ぷ	pe	ぺ	po	ぽ

gya	ぎゃ	gyu	ぎゅ	gyo	ぎょ
ja	じゃ	ju	じゅ	jo	じょ

bya	びゃ	byu	びゅ	byo	びょ
pya	ぴゃ	pyu	ぴゅ	pyo	ぴょ

Chapter 2

Examples and Practice

だい に しょう か た か な か
第 2 章　カタカナを書く

Lesson 1

Trace over the grayed examples, then fill in the exercise squares while referring to the numbers and arrows for instruction.

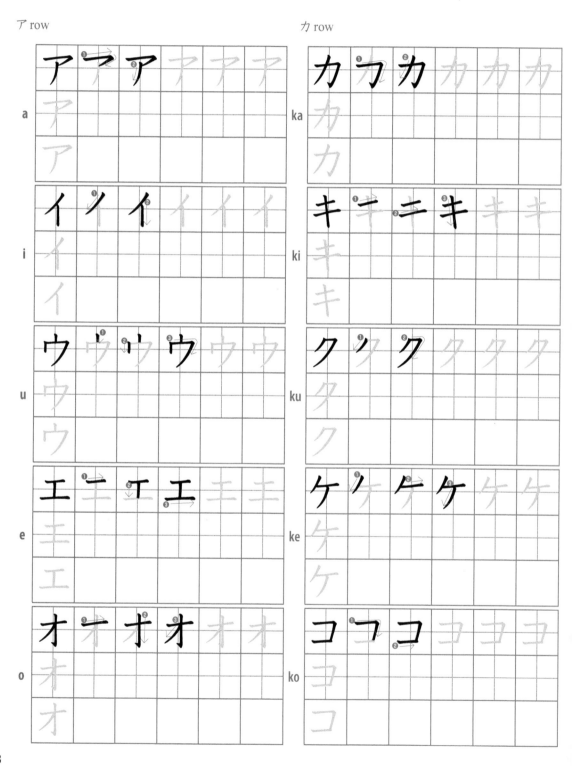

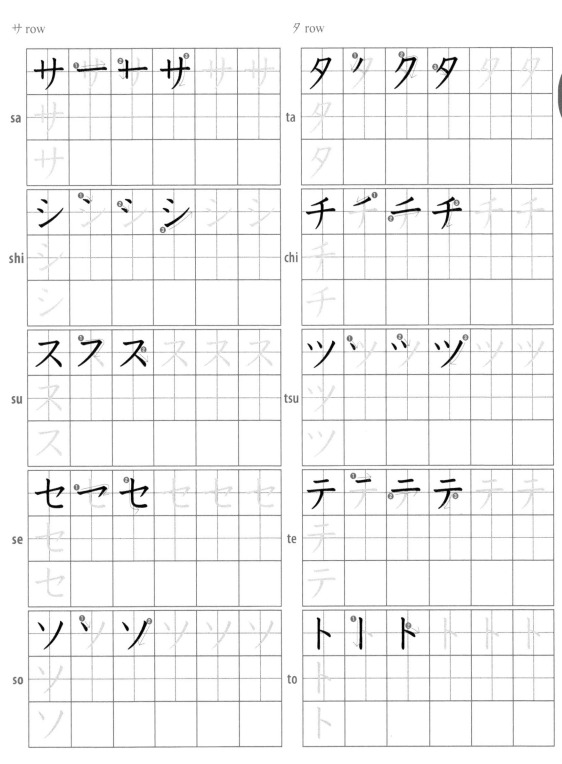

サ row

sa サ

shi シ

su ス

se セ

so ソ

タ row

ta タ

chi チ

tsu ツ

te テ

to ト

2

Trace over the grayed examples, then fill in the exercise squares while referring to the numbers and arrows for instruction.

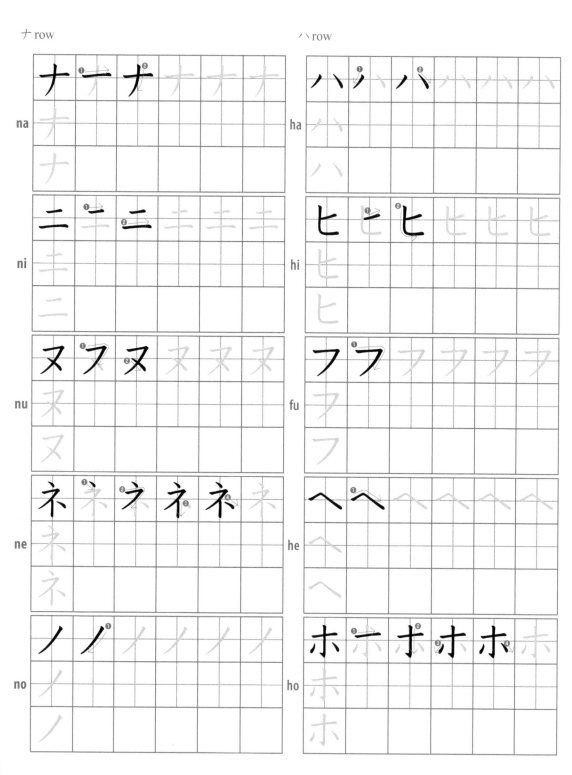

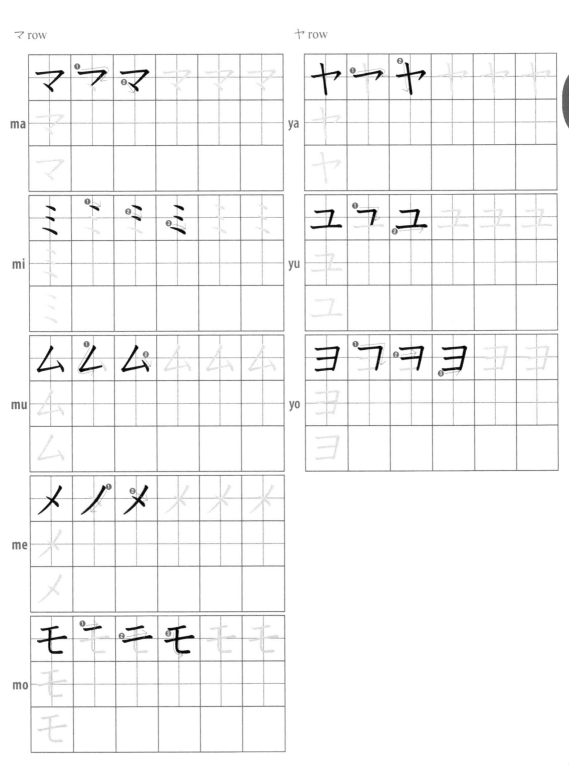

マ row

ma

mi

mu

me

mo

ヤ row

ya

yu

yo

2

Lesson 3

Trace over the grayed examples, then fill in the exercise squares while referring to the numbers and arrows for instruction.

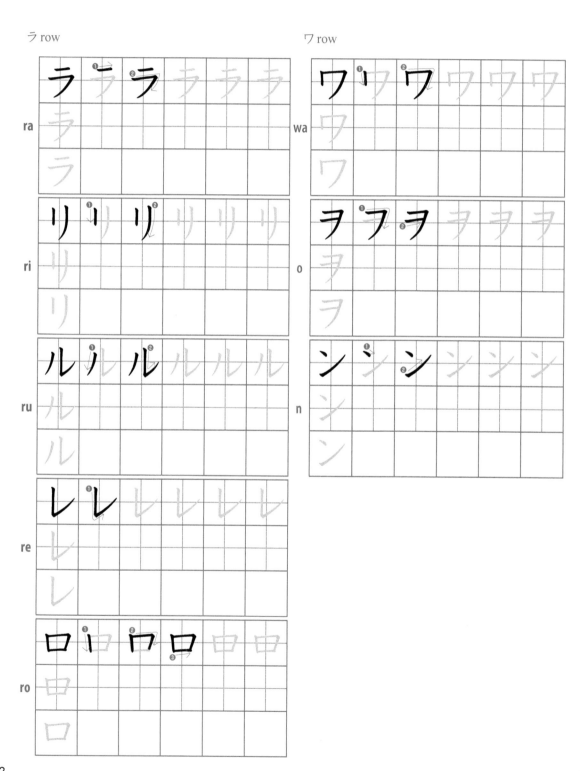

ラ row

ワ row

ra

ri

ru

re

ro

wa

o

n

ガ row

ガ	フ	カ	ガ	ガ	ガ

ga

ギ	一	二	キ	ギ	ギ

gi

グ	ク	ク	グ	グ	グ

gu

ゲ	ゲ	ゲ	ゲ	ゲ	ゲ

ge

ゴ	フ	コ	ゴ	ゴ	ゴ

go

ザ row

ザ	一	十	サ	ザ	ザ

za

ジ	ジ	ジ	シ	ジ	ジ

ji

ズ	フ	ス	ズ	ズ	ズ

zu

ゼ	一	セ	セ	ゼ	ゼ

ze

ゾ	ゾ	ゾ	ゾ	ゾ	ゾ

zo

2

Lesson 4

Trace over the grayed examples, then fill in the exercise squares while referring to the numbers and arrows for instruction.

ダ row　　　　　　　　　　　　　　バ row

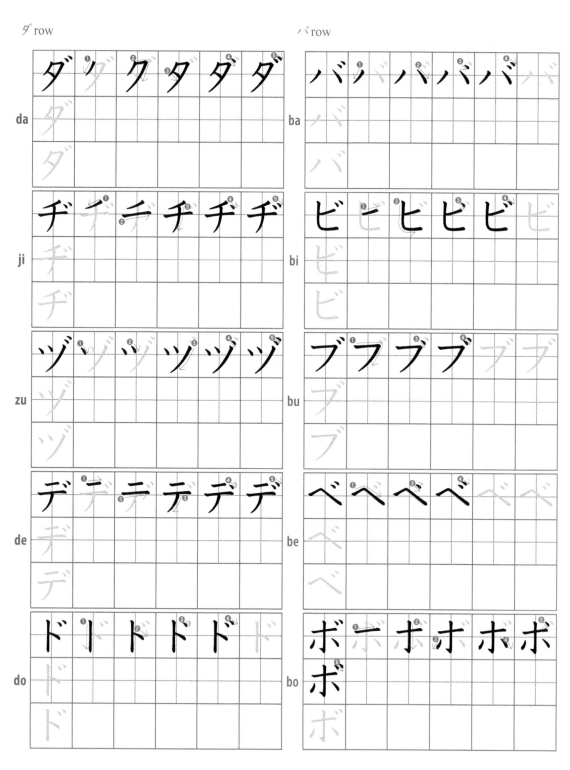

da

ji

zu

de

do

ba

bi

bu

be

bo

パ row

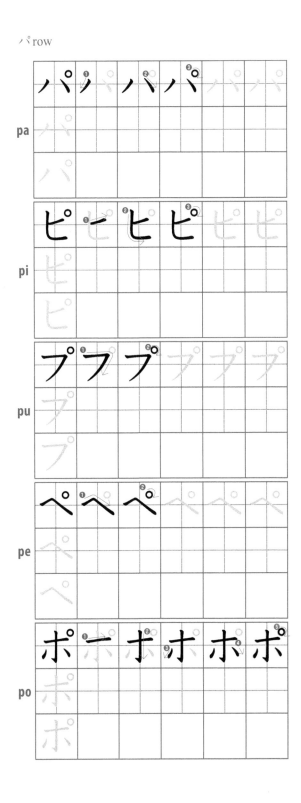

pa

pi

pu

pe

po

Lesson 5

Since the Japanese language does not contain a soft [r] sound, words such as the following are written using the prolonged sound mark.

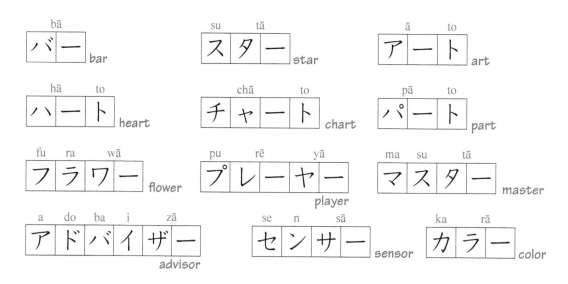

バー bar (bā)	スター star (su tā)	アート art (ā to)
ハート heart (hā to)	チャート chart (chā to)	パート part (pā to)
フラワー flower (fu ra wā)	プレーヤー player (pu rē yā)	マスター master (ma su tā)
アドバイザー advisor (a do ba i zā)	センサー sensor (se n sā)	カラー color (ka rā)

This long mark is also used for the following words.

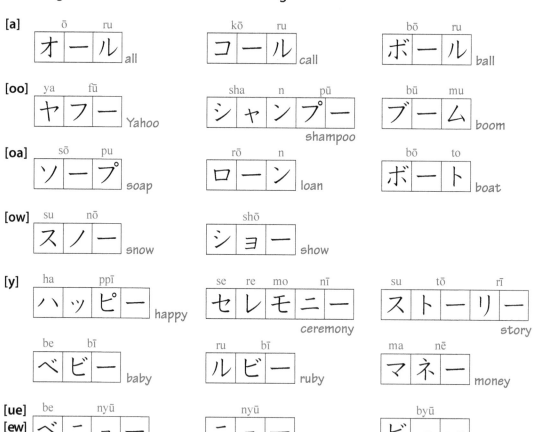

[a]
オール all (ō ru) — コール call (kō ru) — ボール ball (bō ru)

[oo]
ヤフー Yahoo (ya fū) — シャンプー shampoo (sha n pū) — ブーム boom (bū mu)

[oa]
ソープ soap (sō pu) — ローン loan (rō n) — ボート boat (bō to)

[ow]
スノー snow (su nō) — ショー show (shō)

[y]
ハッピー happy (ha ppī) — セレモニー ceremony (se re mo nī) — ストーリー story (su tō rī)
ベビー baby (be bī) — ルビー ruby (ru bī) — マネー money (ma nē)

[ue]
[ew]
ベニュー venue (be nyū) — ニュー new (nyū) — ビュー view (byū)

26

A Translate the English words into katakana.

1 art
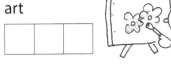

2 part

3 flower

4 boat
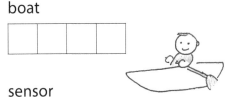

5 sensor

6 Yahoo

2

B Match the following katakana words to their English counter parts.

オール •　　　　　　• snow

ブーム •　　　　　　• ceremony

スノー •　　　　　　• all

ベビー •　　　　　　• baby

セレモニー •　　　　　　• boom

Lesson 6

The small [tsu] (ッ) isn't pronounced—it merely indicates a slight pause before the pronunciation of the following syllable.

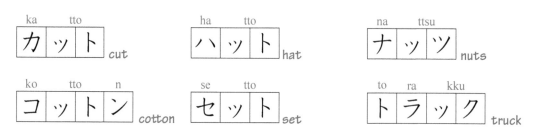

Small vowels (ァ, ィ, ゥ, ェ, ォ) and small "Y" characters (ャ, ュ, ョ) modify the pronunciation of the preceding character by replacing its vowel sound. This allows for the creation of some sounds which are not originally found in Japanese. For example, there is no kana character for approximating the [fi] sound in the English word "fish." But by combining フ with a small ィ, we can replace the [u] vowel sound on the end of フ with the ィ sound (which in Japanese is pronounced like a long [ee] in English).

small アイウエオ

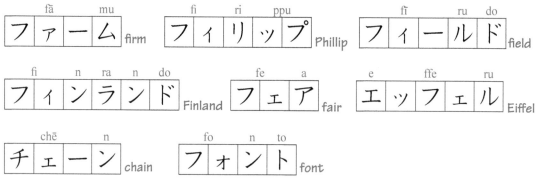

small ヤユヨ

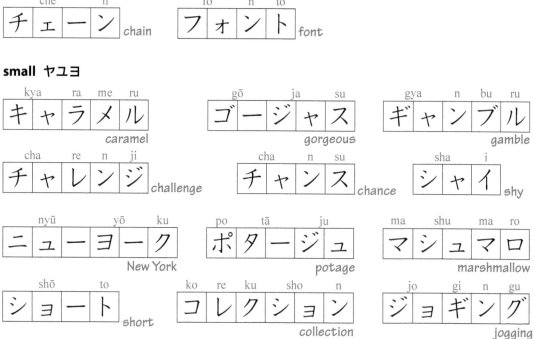

A   Write the following English words in katakana.

1 hat
⬚⬚⬚

4 shy
⬚⬚⬚

2 truck
⬚⬚⬚⬚

5 gamble
⬚⬚⬚⬚⬚

3 font
⬚⬚⬚⬚

6 marshmallow
⬚⬚⬚⬚⬚

B   Match each katakana word to its English equivalent.

コットン　•　　　　　　•　caramel

フィールド　•　　　　　•　cotton

キャラメル　•　　　　　•　collection

チャンス　•　　　　　　•　chance

コレクション　•　　　　•　field

Tricky Characters

These characters have similar shapes, so take extra care when using them.

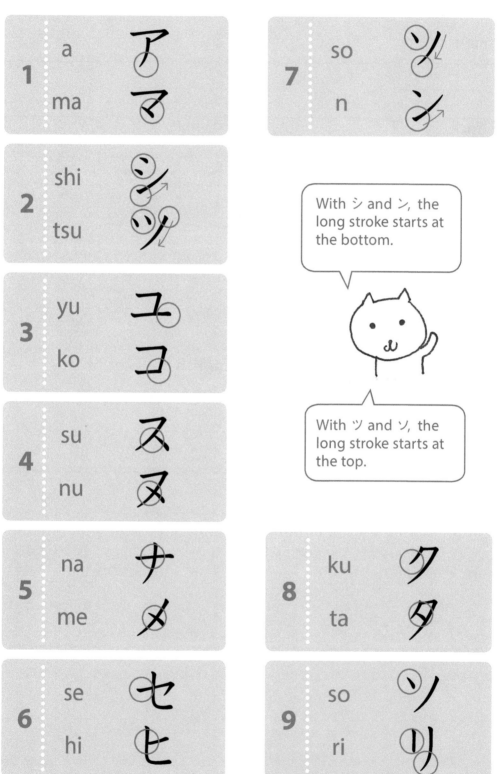

1
  a ア
  ma マ

2
  shi シ
  tsu ツ

3
  yu ユ
  ko コ

4
  su ス
  nu ヌ

5
  na ナ
  me メ

6
  se セ
  hi ヒ

7
  so ソ
  n ン

With シ and ン, the long stroke starts at the bottom.

With ツ and ソ, the long stroke starts at the top.

8
  ku ク
  ta タ

9
  so ソ
  ri リ

Which one is correct?

1 a i su
ᵃ アイス
ᵇ マイス

2 shī tsu
ᵃ ツーシ
ᵇ シーツ

3 pa n da
ᵃ パソダ
ᵇ パンダ

4 sū pu
ᵃ スープ
ᵇ ヌープ

5 ko a ra
ᵃ コアラ
ᵇ ユアラ

6 me ro n
ᵃ ナロン
ᵇ メロン

7 te ni su
ᵃ チニス
ᵇ テニス

8 wa i n
ᵃ ワイン
ᵇ ウイン

Answer : *English*

1　a / *ice cream*　　4　a / *soup*　　　7　b / *tennis*
2　b / *sheets*　　　 5　a / *koala*　　　8　a / *wine*
3　b / *panda*　　　　6　b / *melon*

Chapter 3

Katakana Words

だい さん しょう　　か た か な　　こと ば
第 3 章　カタカナの言葉

Café Drink Menu　カフェ ドリンクメニュー

ka fe do ri n ku me nyū

Since many items found on café menus are direct cultural imports to Japan, you will probably recognize most of them.

Review the katakana words in the picture.

ka fe o re
カフェオレ
café au lait

ka fe ra te
カフェラテ
caffé latte

koko a
ココア
cocoa

a me ri ka n kō hī
アメリカンコーヒー
American coffee

e su pu re sso
エスプレッソ
espresso

ho tto mi ru ku tī
ホットミルクティー
tea with milk

ho tto re mo n tī
ホットレモンティー
tea with lemon

bu re n do kō hī
ブレンドコーヒー
blended coffee

a i su ka fe o re
アイスカフェオレ
iced café au lait

a i su ka fe ra te
アイスカフェラテ
iced caffé latte

kō ra
コーラ
cola

a i su kō hī
アイスコーヒー
iced coffee

kō hī fu rō to
コーヒーフロート
coffee float

o re n ji jū su
オレンジジュース
orange juice

[Exercise 1] Match the katakana to the correct pronunciation.

ブレンドコーヒー　•

エスプレッソ　•

ココア　•

コーヒーフロート　•

オレンジジュース　•

•　e su pu re sso

•　bu re n do kō hī

•　o re n ji jū su

•　kō hī fu rō to

•　ko ko a

[Exercise 2] Practice writing the characters in the boxes provided.

blended coffee

ブ	レ	ン	ド	コ	ー	ヒ	ー

tea with milk

ホ	ッ	ト	ミ	ル	ク	ティ	ー

espresso

エ	ス	プ	レ	ッ	ソ

iced coffee

ア	イ	ス	コ	ー	ヒ	ー

cocoa

コ	コ	ア

café au lait

カ	フ	ェ	オ	レ

cola

コ	ー	ラ

orange juice

オ	レ	ン	ジ	ジ	ュ	ー	ス

3

[Exercise 3] Translate the English words into katakana.

blended coffee

tea with milk

espresso

iced coffee

cocoa

café au lait

cola

orange juice

American coffee

coffee float

tea with lemon

caffé latte

Café Menu　カフェ メニュー
<small>ka　fe　me　nyū</small>

Cafés that serve Western food are very popular in Japan.

**Review the katakana words
in the picture.**

rō ru kē ki
ロールケーキ
roll cake

a ppu ru pa i
アップルパイ
apple pie

kē ki
ケーキ
cake

ku ro wa ssa n
クロワッサン
croissant

dō na tsu
ドーナツ
doughnut

ho tto do ggu
ホットドッグ
hot dog

pa fe
パフェ
parfait

tō su to
トースト
toast

[Exercise 1] Match the katakana to the correct pronunciation.

ロールケーキ　　•

アップルパイ　　•

クロワッサン　　•

ドーナツ　　•

パフェ　　•

•　dō na tsu

•　ku ro wa ssa n

•　rō ru kē ki

•　a ppu ru pa i

•　pa fe

[Exercise 2] Practice writing the characters in the boxes provided.

cake

ケ	ー	キ

roll cake

ロ	ー	ル	ケ	ー	キ

apple pie

ア	ッ	プ	ル	パ	イ

hot dog

ホ	ッ	ト	ド	ッ	グ

toast

ト	ー	ス	ト

croissant

ク	ロ	ワ	ッ	サ	ン

doughnut

ド	ー	ナ	ツ

parfait

パ	フ	エ

[Exercise 3] Translate the English words into katakana.

roll cake

apple pie

hot dog

toast

croissant

doughnut

parfait

Restaurant Menu　<ruby>レストラン メニュー<rt>re su to ra n　me nyū</rt></ruby>

Places that serve *wa-shoku* (traditional Japanese cuisine) will generally have menus written in kanji, but there are also many Western-style restaurants where the menus will appear largely in katakana.

Review the katakana words in the picture.

su pa ge tti
スパゲッティ
spaghetti

o mu ra i su
オムライス
omelet on rice

pa su ta
パスタ
pasta

ka rē　ra i su
カレーライス
curry rice

pi za
ピザ
pizza

ha n　bā gu
ハンバーグ
Salisbury steak

su　tē ki
ステーキ
steak

ra n chi se tto
ランチセット
lunch set

[Exercise 1] Match the katakana to the correct pronunciation.

パスタ・	・ha n bā gu
ハンバーグ・	・o mu ra i su
ステーキ・	・pa su ta
オムライス・	・ka rē ra i su
カレーライス・	・su tē ki

[Exercise 2] Practice writing the characters in the boxes provided.

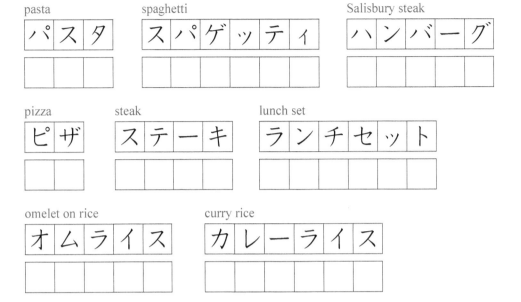

pasta

パ	ス	タ

spaghetti

ス	パ	ゲ	ッ	テ	ィ

Salisbury steak

ハ	ン	バ	ー	グ

pizza

ピ	ザ

steak

ス	テ	ー	キ

lunch set

ラ	ン	チ	セ	ッ	ト

omelet on rice

オ	ム	ラ	イ	ス

curry rice

カ	レ	ー	ラ	イ	ス

[Exercise 3] Translate the English words into katakana.

pasta

spaghetti

Salisbury steak

pizza

steak

lunch set

omelet on rice

curry rice

3

Alcohol　お<ruby>酒<rt>さけ</rt></ruby>

Japan has some unique variations on alcoholic drinks. One popular item is a mixture of Japanese liquor and flavored soda water known as a チューハイ or "shōchū highball."

Review the katakana words in the picture.

wa i n
ワイン
wine

bu ra n dē
ブランデー
brandy

ka ku te ru
カクテル
cocktail

bī ru
ビール
beer

u i su kī
ウイスキー
whisky

u o kka
ウォッカ
vodka

chū ha i
チューハイ
chu-hi

te kī ra
テキーラ
tequila

ji n
ジン
gin

[Exercise 1] Match the katakana to the correct pronunciation.

ビール	•		•	u i su kī
ワイン	•		•	ka ku te ru
カクテル	•		•	wa i n
ウイスキー	•		•	bī ru
チューハイ	•		•	chū ha i

[Exercise 2] Practice writing the characters in the boxes provided.

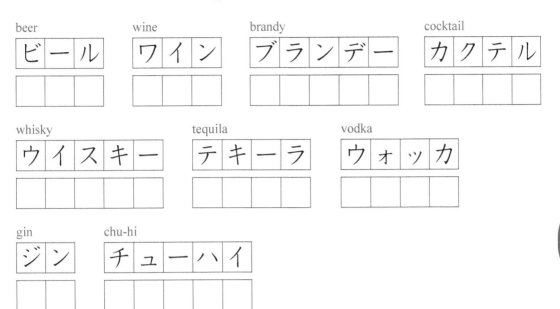

beer

ビ	ー	ル

wine

ワ	イ	ン

brandy

ブ	ラ	ン	デ	ー

cocktail

カ	ク	テ	ル

whisky

ウ	イ	ス	キ	ー

tequila

テ	キ	ー	ラ

vodka

ウ	ォ	ッ	カ

gin

ジ	ン

chu-hi

チ	ュ	ー	ハ	イ

[Exercise 3] Translate the English words into katakana.

beer

wine

brandy

cocktail

whisky

tequila

vodka

gin

chu-hi

Fruits and Vegetables　フルーツと野菜

_{fu rū tsu}　_{ya sai}

These terms will be fairly obvious to an English native speaker, with a few notable exceptions: ピーマン is derived from the French word for green bell pepper (piment), and サニーレタス refers to a type of red-leaf lettuce commonly sold in Japan.

Review the katakana words in the picture.

pa i na ppu ru
パイナップル
pineapple

ki u i
キウイ
kiwi

o re n ji
オレンジ
orange

a bo ka do
アボカド
avocado

ba na na
バナナ
banana

sa nī re ta su
サニーレタス
red-leaf lettuce

bu ro kko rī
ブロッコリー
broccoli

me ro n
メロン
melon

pī ma n
ピーマン
bell pepper

to ma to
トマト
tomato

kya be tsu
キャベツ
cabbage

[Exercise 1] Match the katakana to the correct pronunciation.

バナナ　・　　　　　　・　ba na na

オレンジ　・　　　　　　・　to ma to

サニーレタス　・　　　　　　・　o re n ji

トマト　・　　　　　　・　kya be tsu

キャベツ　・　　　　　　・　sa nī re ta su

[Exercise 2] Practice writing the characters in the boxes provided.

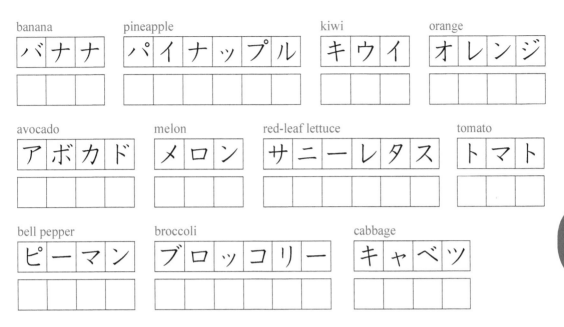

banana
バ	ナ	ナ

pineapple
パ	イ	ナ	ッ	プ	ル

kiwi
キ	ウ	イ

orange
オ	レ	ン	ジ

avocado
ア	ボ	カ	ド

melon
メ	ロ	ン

red-leaf lettuce
サ	ニ	ー	レ	タ	ス

tomato
ト	マ	ト

bell pepper
ピ	ー	マ	ン

broccoli
ブ	ロ	ッ	コ	リ	ー

cabbage
キ	ャ	ベ	ツ

[Exercise 3] Translate the English words into katakana.

banana

pineapple

kiwi

orange

avocado

melon

red-leaf lettuce

bell pepper

broccoli

tomato

cabbage

Ramen Shop ラーメン屋

Many of these words were imported from Chinese and have corresponding pronunciations. Although each term can also be represented using kanji, katakana is widely used instead because it is easier to read.

Review the katakana words in the picture.

ne gi
ネギ
green onion

shū ma i
シューマイ
dumpling

gyō za
ギョーザ
jiaozi (Chinese dumplings)

me n ma
メンマ
boiled bamboo shoots

chā shū
チャーシュー
char siu (sliced pork)

na ru to
ナルト
naruto

rā me n
ラーメン
ramen

ra i su
ライス
rice

chā ha n
チャーハン
fried rice

sū pu
スープ
soup

[Exercise 1] Match the katakana to the correct pronunciation.

チャーハン　•

ラーメン　•

ネギ　•

シューマイ　•

ライス　•

•　rā me n

•　chā ha n

•　shū ma i

•　ne gi

•　ra i su

[Exercise 2] Practice writing the characters in the boxes provided.

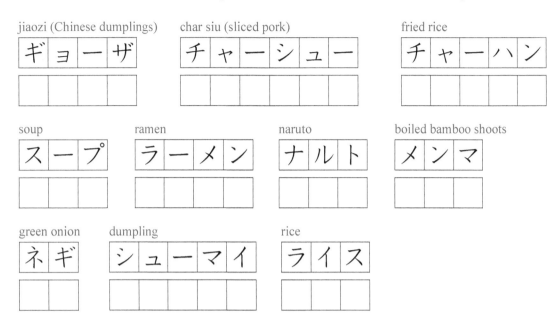

jiaozi (Chinese dumplings)

ギョーザ

char siu (sliced pork)

チャーシュー

fried rice

チャーハン

soup

スープ

ramen

ラーメン

naruto

ナルト

boiled bamboo shoots

メンマ

green onion

ネギ

dumpling

シューマイ

rice

ライス

[Exercise 3] Translate the English words into katakana.

jiaozi (Chinese dumplings)

char siu (sliced pork)

soup

ramen

naruto

green onion

dumpling

rice

boiled bamboo shoots

Foods　食^たべもの

Since ingredients like チーズ and バター were not traditionally used in Japanese cuisine, there are no kanji to represent them and they aren't written in hiragana. マヨネーズ is very popular in Japan and is often shortened to マヨ.

Review the katakana words in the picture.

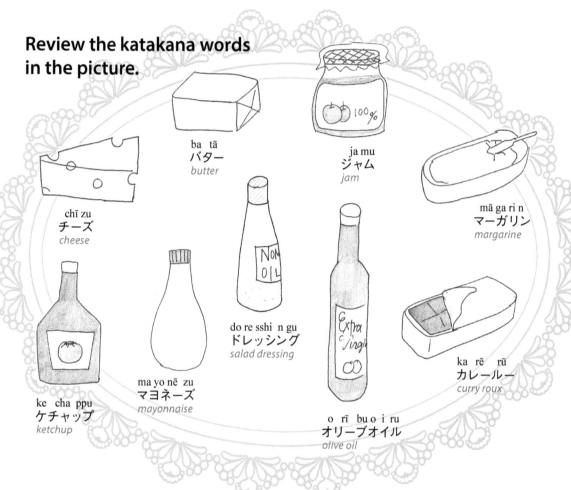

ba tā
バター
butter

ja mu
ジャム
jam

mā ga ri n
マーガリン
margarine

chī zu
チーズ
cheese

do re sshi n gu
ドレッシング
salad dressing

ka rē rū
カレールー
curry roux

ke cha ppu
ケチャップ
ketchup

ma yo nē zu
マヨネーズ
mayonnaise

o rī bu o i ru
オリーブオイル
olive oil

[Exercise 1] Match the katakana to the correct pronunciation.

チーズ　・   ・　ma yo nē zu

マーガリン　・   ・　do re sshi n gu

マヨネーズ　・   ・　ka rē rū

ドレッシング　・   ・　mā ga ri n

カレールー　・   ・　chī zu

[Exercise 2] Practice writing the characters in the boxes provided.

cheese
チ	ー	ズ

butter
バ	タ	ー

jam
ジ	ャ	ム

margarine
マ	ー	ガ	リ	ン

ketchup
ケ	チ	ャ	ッ	プ

mayonnaise
マ	ヨ	ネ	ー	ズ

salad dressing
ド	レ	ッ	シ	ン	グ

olive oil
オ	リ	ー	ブ	オ	イ	ル

curry roux
カ	レ	ー	ル	ー

[Exercise 3] Translate the English words into katakana.

cheese

butter

jam

margarine

ketchup

mayonnaise

salad dressing

olive oil

curry roux

Kitchen　キッチン
<small>ki　tchi　n</small>

Terms for describing kitchen appliances are largely imported from other languages, but be careful: some of them are completely different than their English counterparts, such as レンジ and ガステーブル.

Review the katakana words in the picture.

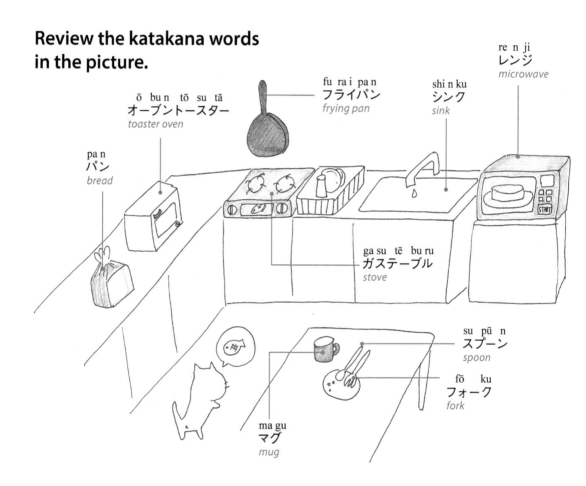

pa n
パン
bread

ō bu n tō su tā
オーブントースター
toaster oven

fu ra i pa n
フライパン
frying pan

shi n ku
シンク
sink

re n ji
レンジ
microwave

ga su tē bu ru
ガステーブル
stove

su pū n
スプーン
spoon

fō ku
フォーク
fork

ma gu
マグ
mug

[Exercise 1] Match the katakana to the correct pronunciation.

パン　　　•　　　　　　•　ga su tē bu ru

フライパン　•　　　　　　•　re n ji

ガステーブル　•　　　　　•　pa n

レンジ　　•　　　　　　　•　fō ku

フォーク　•　　　　　　　•　fu ra i pa n

[Exercise 2] Practice writing the characters in the boxes provided.

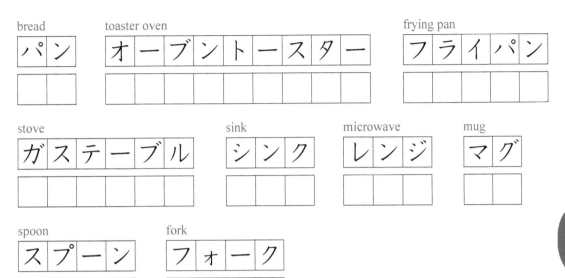

bread
パ	ン

toaster oven
オ	ー	ブ	ン	ト	ー	ス	タ	ー

frying pan
フ	ラ	イ	パ	ン

stove
ガ	ス	テ	ー	ブ	ル

sink
シ	ン	ク

microwave
レ	ン	ジ

mug
マ	グ

spoon
ス	プ	ー	ン

fork
フ	ォ	ー	ク

[Exercise 3] Translate the English words into katakana.

bread

toaster oven

frying pan

stove

sink

microwave

mug

spoon

fork

(Bed)room　部屋(へや)

Almost all of these terms are direct English imports, although the Japanese like to abbreviate them; スマートホン becomes スマホ, パーソナル・コンピューター becomes パソコン, etc.

Review the katakana words in the picture.

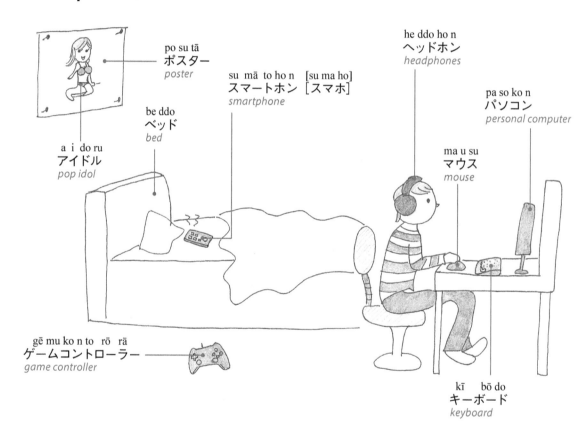

po su tā
ポスター
poster

su mā to ho n　[su ma ho]
スマートホン［スマホ］
smartphone

he ddo ho n
ヘッドホン
headphones

pa so ko n
パソコン
personal computer

be ddo
ベッド
bed

ma u su
マウス
mouse

a i do ru
アイドル
pop idol

gē mu ko n to rō rā
ゲームコントローラー
game controller

kī　bō do
キーボード
keyboard

[Exercise 1] Match the katakana to the correct pronunciation.

アイドル　•	•　a i do ru
ベッド　•	•　su mā to ho n
スマートホン　•	•　pa so ko n
キーボード　•	•　kī bō do
パソコン　•	•　be ddo

[Exercise 2] Practice writing the characters in the boxes provided.

pop idol

ア	イ	ド	ル

poster

ポ	ス	タ	ー

bed

ベ	ッ	ド

smartphone

ス	マ	ー	ト	ホ	ン

headphones

ヘ	ッ	ド	ホ	ン

game controller

ゲ	ー	ム	コ	ン	ト	ロ	ー	ラ	ー

keyboard

キ	ー	ボ	ー	ド

mouse

マ	ウ	ス

personal computer

パ	ソ	コ	ン

[Exercise 3] Translate the English words into katakana.

pop idol

poster

bed

personal computer

smartphone

game controller

headphones

keyboard

mouse

Lesson 16

Living Room　リビング

<small>ri bi n gu</small>

Modern Japanese homes have been Westernized to a large extent, and traditional tatami rooms are becoming scarce. As a result, many items found in these rooms are described using imported words.

Review the katakana words in the picture.

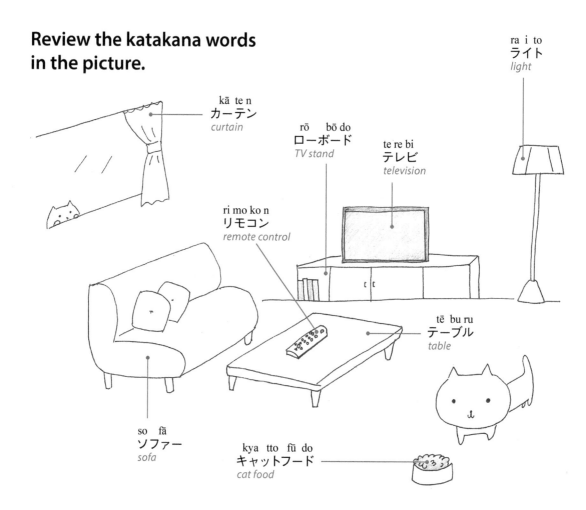

ra i to
ライト
light

kā te n
カーテン
curtain

rō bō do
ローボード
TV stand

te re bi
テレビ
television

ri mo ko n
リモコン
remote control

tē bu ru
テーブル
table

so fā
ソファー
sofa

kya tto fū do
キャットフード
cat food

[Exercise 1] Match the katakana to the correct pronunciation.

カーテン　•	• 　tē bu ru
テレビ　•	• 　te re bi
リモコン　•	• 　kā te n
テーブル　•	• 　ri mo ko n
ライト　•	• 　ra i to

[Exercise 2] Practice writing the characters in the boxes provided.

curtain

カ	ー	テ	ン

sofa

ソ	フ	ァ	ー

TV stand

ロ	ー	ボ	ー	ド

television

テ	レ	ビ

remote control

リ	モ	コ	ン

table

テ	ー	ブ	ル

cat food

キ	ャ	ッ	ト	フ	ー	ド

light

ラ	イ	ト

[Exercise 3] Translate the English words into katakana.

curtain

sofa

TV stand

remote control

table

cat food

light

television

Convenience Store コンビニ
<small>ko n bi ni</small>

Much of the food found in convenience stores is described using terms that will be familiar to English speakers, but take note of the few oddities such as レジ and トイレ. The word コンビニエンス itself is usually shortened to コンビニ.

Review the katakana words in the picture.

sa n do i tchi
サンドイッチ
sandwich

yō gu ru to
ヨーグルト
yogurt

pu ri n
プリン
pudding

a i su (ku rī m
アイス（クリーム
ice cream

ga mu
ガム
gum

cho ko rē to
チョコレート
chocolate

po te to chi ppu su
ポテトチップス
potato chips

re ji
レジ
cash register

ko pī
コピー
copy machine

to i re
トイレ
restroom

[Exercise 1] Match the katakana to the correct pronunciation.

レジ	•	•	ga mu
コピー	•	•	sa n do i tchi
ガム	•	•	ko pī
トイレ	•	•	to i re
サンドイッチ	•	•	re ji

[Exercise 2] Practice writing the characters in the boxes provided.

cash register

レ	ジ

copy machine

コ	ピ	ー

chocolate

チ	ョ	コ	レ	ー	ト

gum

ガ	ム

potato chips

ポ	テ	ト	チ	ッ	プ	ス

ice cream

ア	イ	ス	ク	リ	ー	ム

rest room

ト	イ	レ

sandwich

サ	ン	ド	イ	ッ	チ

yogurt

ヨ	ー	グ	ル	ト

pudding

プ	リ	ン

[Exercise 3] Translate the English words into katakana.

cash register

copy machine

chocolate

gum

potato chips

ice cream

sandwich

yogurt

pudding

Drugstore　ドラッグストア
do ra ggu su to a

These everyday items are not new to Japan and they do have corresponding Japanese terms, but nowadays they are expressed using katakana. This gives them a more modern and fashionable impression.

Review the katakana words in the picture.

to i re tto pē pā
トイレットペーパー
toilet paper

o mu tsu
オムツ
diaper

be bī fū do
ベビーフード
baby food

ti sshu
ティッシュ
tissues

sha n pū
シャンプー
shampoo

ko n di sho nā
コンディショナー
conditioner

ha n do ku rī mu
ハンドクリーム
hand cream

sa pu ri me n to
サプリメント
supplement

ko su me
コスメ
cosmetic

[Exercise 1] Match the katakana to the correct pronunciation.

トイレットペーパー　・ ・ o mu tsu

オムツ　・ ・ to i re tto pē pā

シャンプー　・ ・ sa pu ri me n to

コスメ　・ ・ ko su me

サプリメント　・ ・ sha n pū

[Exercise 2] Practice writing the characters in the boxes provided.

toilet paper

ト	イ	レ	ッ	ト	ペ	ー	パ	ー

diaper

オ	ム	ツ

cosmetic

コ	ス	メ

tissues

テ	ィ	ッ	シ	ュ

baby food

ベ	ビ	ー	フ	ー	ド

shampoo

シ	ャ	ン	プ	ー

conditioner

コ	ン	ディ	ィ	シ	ョ	ナ	ー

lip cream

リ	ッ	プ	ク	リ	ー	ム

hand cream

ハ	ン	ド	ク	リ	ー	ム

supplement

サ	プ	リ	メ	ン	ト

3

[Exercise 3] Translate the English words into katakana.

toilet paper

baby food

tissues

hand cream

conditioner

diaper

shampoo

cosmetic

lip cream

supplement

Fashion　ファッション
<small>fa ssho n</small>

As traditional Japanese clothing was worn up until the dawn of the Meiji period, these words are all imported from English. Fashion magazines and catalogs almost always use katakana to describe these sorts of items.

Review the katakana words in the picture.

ma fu rā
マフラー
muffler

ha n ka chi
ハンカチ
handkerchief

ne ku ta i
ネクタイ
necktie

ja ke tto
ジャケット
jacket

sē tā
セーター
sweater

su kā to
スカート
skirt

ba ggu
バッグ
bag

sū tsu
スーツ
suit

rō fā
ローファー
loafers

ha i hī ru
ハイヒール
high heels

[Exercise 1] Match the katakana to the correct pronunciation.

セーター　•	•　sū tsu
スカート　•	•　su kā to
ジャケット　•	•　ba ggu
バッグ　•	•　ja ke tto
スーツ　•	•　sē tā

[Exercise 2] Practice writing the characters in the boxes provided.

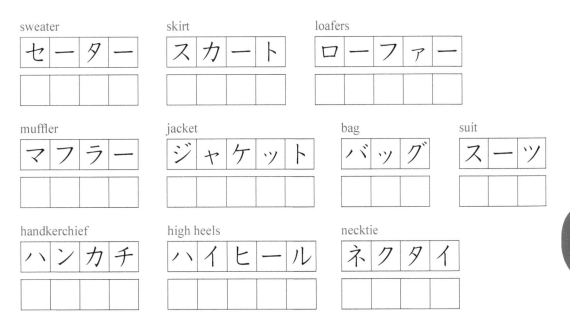

sweater
セ	ー	タ	ー

skirt
ス	カ	ー	ト

loafers
ロ	ー	フ	ァ	ー

muffler
マ	フ	ラ	ー

jacket
ジ	ャ	ケ	ッ	ト

bag
バ	ッ	グ

suit
ス	ー	ツ

handkerchief
ハ	ン	カ	チ

high heels
ハ	イ	ヒ	ー	ル

necktie
ネ	ク	タ	イ

[Exercise 3] Translate the English words into katakana.

sweater

skirt

loafers

muffler

jacket

high heels

bag

handkerchief

suit

necktie

Lesson 20

Sports　スポーツ
su pō tsu

Sports like judo and karate which originated in Japan have their own kanji, but most others are written in katakana. Abbreviations such as バスケ for バスケットボール and バレー for バレーボール are also common.

Review the katakana words in the picture.

ba su ke tto bō ru
バスケットボール
basketball

ba rē bō ru
バレーボール
volleyball

su kī
スキー
skiing

go ru fu
ゴルフ
golf

ra n ni n gu
ランニング
running

te ni su
テニス
tennis

sa kkā
サッカー
soccer

fi gyu a su kē to
フィギュアスケート
figure skating

[Exercise 1] Match the katakana to the correct pronunciation.

バスケットボール ・	・ fi gyu a su kē to
テニス ・	・ go ru fu
サッカー ・	・ sa kkā
フィギュアスケート ・	・ te ni su
ゴルフ ・	・ ba su ke tto bō ru

[Exercise 2] Practice writing the characters in the boxes provided.

basketball

バ	ス	ケ	ッ	ト	ボ	ー	ル

volleyball

バ	レ	ー	ボ	ー	ル

tennis

テ	ニ	ス

soccer

サ	ッ	カ	ー

figure skating

フ	ィ	ギ	ュ	ア	ス	ケ	ー	ト

skiing

ス	キ	ー

running

ラ	ン	ニ	ン	グ

golf

ゴ	ル	フ

[Exercise 3] Translate the English words into katakana.

basketball

volleyball

tennis

soccer

figure skating

skiing

running

golf

3

Lesson 21

Automobiles　車<ruby>くるま</ruby>

Automobile-related terms are all written in katakana, but for some reason they often differ from their English equivalents.

Review the katakana words in the picture.

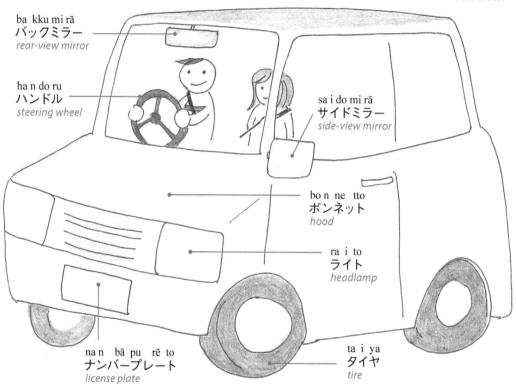

bu rē ki
● ブレーキ
brake

a ku se ru
● アクセル
accelerator

ba kku mi rā
バックミラー
rear-view mirror

ha n do ru
ハンドル
steering wheel

sa i do mi rā
サイドミラー
side-view mirror

bo n ne tto
ボンネット
hood

ra i to
ライト
headlamp

na n bā pu rē to
ナンバープレート
license plate

ta i ya
タイヤ
tire

[Exercise 1] Match the katakana to the correct pronunciation.

ハンドル　•

バックミラー　•

ナンバープレート　•

ブレーキ　•

アクセル　•

•　na n bā pu rē to

•　a ku se ru

•　bu rē ki

•　ha n do ru

•　ba kku mi rā

[Exercise 2] Practice writing the characters in the boxes provided.

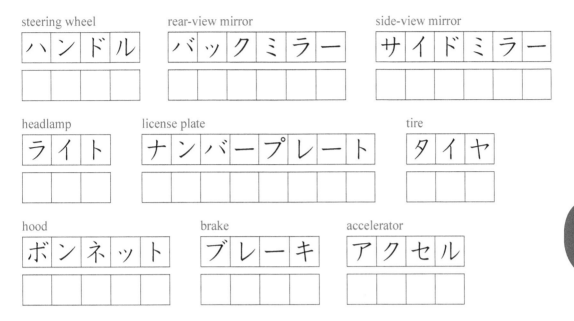

steering wheel

ハ	ン	ド	ル

rear-view mirror

バ	ッ	ク	ミ	ラ	ー

side-view mirror

サ	イ	ド	ミ	ラ	ー

headlamp

ラ	イ	ト

license plate

ナ	ン	バ	ー	プ	レ	ー	ト

tire

タ	イ	ヤ

hood

ボ	ン	ネ	ッ	ト

brake

ブ	レ	ー	キ

accelerator

ア	ク	セ	ル

[Exercise 3] Translate the English words into katakana.

steering wheel

rear-view mirror

side-view mirror

headlamp

license plate

tire

hood

brake

accelerator

Around Town　町の中

Though ビジネスホテル were originally created for company employees on business trips, they have become popular among normal travelers as well due to their low cost and convenience.

Review the katakana words in the picture.

de pā to
デパート
department store

bi ji ne su ho te ru
ビジネスホテル
budget hotel

pā ki n gu
パーキング
parking lot

ho te ru
ホテル
hotel

fu ro n to
フロント
reception

ku rī ni n gu
クリーニング
laundromat

sū pā
スーパー
supermarket

ga so ri n su ta n do
ガソリンスタンド
gas station

[Exercise 1] Match the katakana to the correct pronunciation.

ビジネスホテル	•	• ga so ri n su ta n do
フロント	•	• fu ro n to
ガソリンスタンド	•	• de pā to
スーパー	•	• bi ji ne su ho te ru
デパート	•	• sū pā

[Exercise 2] Practice writing the characters in the boxes provided.

hotel

ホ	テ	ル

budget hotel

ビ	ジ	ネ	ス	ホ	テ	ル

reception

フ	ロ	ン	ト

gas station

ガ	ソ	リ	ン	ス	タ	ン	ド

laundromat

ク	リ	ー	ニ	ン	グ

supermarket

ス	ー	パ	ー

department store

デ	パ	ー	ト

parking lot

パ	ー	キ	ン	グ

[Exercise 3] Translate the English words into katakana.

hotel

budget hotel

reception

gas station

laundromat

supermarket

department store

parking lot

Advertisements 広告
<small>こうこく</small>

Katakana is widely used in advertisements because it gives a more enjoyable impression than hiragana or kanji.

Review the katakana words in the picture.

[Exercise 1] Match the katakana to the correct pronunciation.

セール •	• fe a
オープン •	• ō pu n
キャンペーン •	• sē ru
フェア •	• kya n pē n
ブランド •	• bu ra n do

[Exercise 2] Practice writing the characters in the boxes provided.

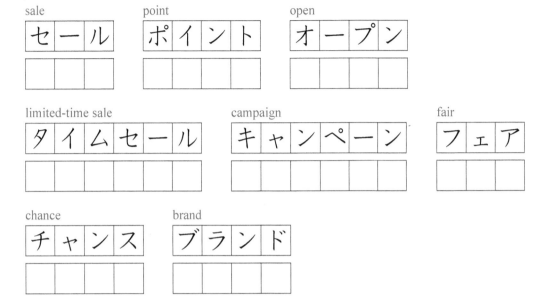

sale

セ	ー	ル

point

ポ	イ	ン	ト

open

オ	ー	プ	ン

limited-time sale

タ	イ	ム	セ	ー	ル

campaign

キ	ャ	ン	ペ	ー	ン

fair

フ	ェ	ア

chance

チ	ャ	ン	ス

brand

ブ	ラ	ン	ド

[Exercise 3] Translate the English words into katakana.

sale

point

open

limited-time sale

campaign

fair

chance

brand

Instruments 楽器
がっき

Just as with sports, traditional Japanese instruments (*taiko*, *koto*, *shakuhachi*, etc.) have their own kanji, while katakana is used for instruments which were introduced to Japan from abroad.

Review the katakana words in the picture.

to ra n pe tto
トランペット
trumpet

to ro n bō n
トロンボーン
trombone

sa kku su
サックス
saxophone

do ra mu
ドラム
drum

gi tā
ギター
guitar

pi a no
ピアノ
piano

bē su
ベース
bass

ba n do
バンド
band

[Exercise 1] Match the katakana to the correct pronunciation.

ピアノ •	• do ra mu
ギター •	• gi tā
ドラム •	• pi a no
サックス •	• sa kku su
バンド •	• ba n do

[Exercise 2] Practice writing the characters in the boxes provided.

piano
ピ	ア	ノ

guitar
ギ	タ	ー

drum
ド	ラ	ム

bass
ベ	ー	ス

trombone
ト	ロ	ン	ボ	ー	ン

trumpet
ト	ラ	ン	ペ	ッ	ト

saxophone
サ	ッ	ク	ス

band
バ	ン	ド

[Exercise 3] Translate the English words into katakana.

piano

guitar

drum

bass

trombone

trumpet

saxophone

band

Chapter 4

People, Places, and Business

第4章　人・場所・ビジネスに
関するカタカナ

Countries　国名
<ruby>こくめい</ruby>

Though a few country names like イギリス and ドイツ have pronunciations that differ significantly from English, many of them will be quite recognizable when spoken. But because Japanese syllables are relatively unstressed, long words such as オーストラリア and ウズベキスタン can be tricky for foreigners to pronounce.

アイスランド a i su ra n do *Iceland*	ウズベキスタン u zu be ki su ta n *Uzbekistan*	ケニア ke ni a *Kenya*
アフガニスタン a fu ga ni su ta n *Afghanistan*	エジプト e ji pu to *Egypt*	コロンビア ko ro n bi a *Colombia*
アメリカ a me ri ka *United States*	エチオピア e chi o pi a *Ethiopia*	サウジアラビア sa u ji a ra bi a *Saudi Arabia*
アルゼンチン a ru ze n chi n *Argentina*	オーストラリア ō su to ra ri a *Australia*	シリア shi ri a *Syria*
イギリス i gi ri su *England*	オーストリア ō su to ri a *Austria*	シンガポール shi n ga pō ru *Singapore*
イタリア i ta ri a *Italy*	オランダ o ra n da *Holland / Netherlands*	スーダン sū da n *Sudan*
インド i n do *India*	ガーナ gā na *Ghana*	スイス su i su *Switzerland*
インドネシア in do ne shi a *Indonesia*	カナダ ka na da *Canada*	スウェーデン su wē de n *Sweden*
イラン i ra n *Iran*	キューバ kyū ba *Cuba*	スペイン su pe i n *Spain*
ウガンダ u ga n da *Uganda*	ギリシャ gi ri sha *Greece*	スリランカ su ri ra n ka *Sri Lanka*
ウクライナ u ku ra i na *Ukraine*	クウェート ku wē to *Kuwait*	ソマリア so ma ri a *Somalia*

タイ ta i *Thailand*	フィジー fi jī *Fiji*	ベルギー be ru gī *Belgium*
チリ chi ri *Chile*	フィリピン fi ri pi n *Philippines*	ポーランド pō ra n do *Poland*
デンマーク de n mā ku *Denmark*	フィンランド fi n ra n do *Finland*	マダガスカル ma da ga su ka ru *Madagascar*
ドイツ do i tsu *Germany*	プエルトリコ pu e ru to ri ko *Puerto Rico*	メキシコ me ki shi ko *Mexico*
トルコ to ru ko *Turkey*	ブラジル bu ra ji ru *Brazil*	モロッコ mo ro kko *Morocco*
ニュージーランド nyū jī ra n do *New Zealand*	フランス fu ra n su *France*	ルワンダ ru wa n da *Rwanda*
ノルウェー no ru wē *Norway*	ベトナム be to na mu *Vietnam*	ロシア ro shi a *Russia*
パラオ pa ra o *Palau*	ペルー pe rū *Peru*	

Lesson 26

English Names 英語名
<ruby>英<rt>えい</rt>語<rt>ご</rt>名<rt>めい</rt></ruby>

Japanese has a small number of unique syllables, which can make it difficult to accurately express your own name in katakana. It is a good idea to practice until you can read and write your own name quickly, however.

アレキサンダー
a re ki san dā
Alexander

アン
a n
Ann

アンディ
a n di
Andy

イアン
i a n
Ian

エイドリアン
e i do ri an
Adrian

エリック
e ri kku
Eric

オリヴィア
o ri bi a
Olivia

クリス
ku ri su
Chris

クリスティーヌ
ku ri su tī nu
Christina

ケイト
ke i to
Kate

サリー
sa rī
Sally

スーザン
sū za n
Susan

ソフィア
so fi a
Sophia

トム
to mu
Tom

ジェシー
je shī
Jesse

ジョーン
jō n
Joan

ジョン
jo n
John

タイラー
ta i rā
Tyler

ナタリー na ta rī *Natalie*	モニカ mo ni ka *Monica*
ビリー bi rī *Billy*	ライアン ra i a n *Ryan*
ヘンリー he n rī *Henry*	ルーク rū ku *Luke*
マイク ma i ku *Mike*	レベッカ re be kka *Rebecca*
マルタ ma ru ta *Marta*	ロバート ro bā to *Robert*
ミッシェル mi sshe ru *Michelle*	ワイアット wa i a tto *Wyatt*

Companies　会社名
_{かいしゃめい}

Katakana is not just used for the names of foreign companies. Japanese companies often use it often as well because it has a more obvious pronunciation than kanji and works well as a company logo.

アウディ a u di *Audi*	キヤノン kya no n *Canon*
アサヒ a sa hi *Asahi*	キリン ki ri n *Kirin*
アップル a ppu ru *Apple*	グーグル gū gu ru *Google*
アマゾン a ma zo n *Amazon*	グッチ gu tchi *Gucci*
イケア i ke a *Ikea*	ケロッグ ke ro ggu *Kellogg*
インテル i n te ru *Intel*	サムスン sa mu su n *Samsung*
エルメス e ru me su *Hermes*	サントリー sa n to rī *Suntory*
オラクル o ra ku ru *Oracle*	シャープ shā pu *Sharp*

スズキ
su zu ki
Suzuki

ソフトバンク
so fu to ba n ku
SoftBank

トヨタ
to yo ta
Toyota

ネスレ
ne su re
Nestle

パナソニック
pa na so ni kku
Panasonic

フォード
fō do
Ford

フォルクスワーゲン
fo ru ku su wā ge n
Volkswagen

ボーイング
bō i n gu
Boeing

ホンダ
ho n da
Honda

マツダ
ma tsu da
Mazda

ヤマハ
ya ma ha
Yamaha

ユニクロ
yu ni ku ro
Uniqlo

ルイ・ヴィトン
ru i bi to n
Louis Vuitton

4

V is written as ヴ but pronunced with a [b] sound.

Business Terms　ビジネス用語

<ruby>bi ji ne su よう ご</ruby>

Due to the effects of globalization, katakana is now often used to express English words. But true English pronunciations can sometimes be difficult for Japanese people to understand, so if you use them try to speak in a slow, even tone.

アジェンダ
a je n da
agenda

アポ
a po
appointment

アライアンス
a ra i a n su
alliance

イニシアチブ
i ni shi a chi bu
initiative

イノベーション
i no bē sho n
innovation

インターフェース
i n tā fē su
interface

ウィンウィン
wi n wi n
win-win

キャパ
kya pa
capacity

キャンセル
kya n se ru
cancel

クライアント
ku ra i a n to
client

クラウド
ku ra u do
cloud

コンセプト
ko n se pu to
concept

コンセンサス
ko n se n sa su
consensus

コンピテンシー
ko n pi te n shī
competency

シナジー
shi na jī
synergy

スキーム
su kī mu
scheme

スケジュール
su ke jū ru
schedule

タイト
ta i to
tight

タスク
ta su ku
task

フェーズ
fē zu
phase

ブラッシュアップ
bu ra sshu a ppu
brush up

プロジェクト
pu ro je ku to
project

マイルストーン
ma i ru su tō n
milestone

ミーティング
mī ti n gu
meeting

モデリング
mo de ri n gu
modeling

ワークショップ
wā ku sho ppu
workshop

4

Katakana words borrowed
from English are heavily used
in Japanese business.

Computer Terms コンピューター用語
ko n pyū tā ようご

Virtually all terms related to computers are loanwords and thus written in katakana, but be careful with some of the incongruous pronunciations like アプリ and ルーター.

アイコン
a i ko n
icon

アカウント
a ka u n to
account

アプリ
a pu ri
app

インストール
i n su tō ru
install

ウイルス
u i ru su
virus

オフライン
o fu ra i n
offline

オンライン
o n ra i n
online

カーソル
kā so ru
cursor

サーバー
sā bā
server

スペック
su pe kku
spec(ification)

ダウンロード
da u n rō do
download

タスクバー
ta su ku bā
taskbar

チャット
cha tto
chat

ドメイン
do me i n
domain

ハッカー
ha kkā
hacker

バナー
ba nā
banner

ファイル
fa i ru
file

モデム
mo de mu
modem

ブックマーク
bu kku mā ku
bookmark

ユーザーネーム
yū zā nē mu
username

ブラウザ
bu ra u za
browser

ライブラリ
ra i bu ra ri
library

プロバイダ
pu ro ba i da
provider

リンク
ri n ku
link

ポインター
po i n tā
pointer

ルーター
rū tā
router

マウス
ma u su
mouse

レス
re su
response

メール
mē ru
email

Chapter 5

Wasei-Eigo and Other Terms

第 5 章　和製英語など

Lesson 30

Wasei-Eigo 1　和製英語 1
<ruby>和<rt>わ</rt>製<rt>せい</rt>英<rt>えい</rt>語<rt>ご</rt></ruby> <ruby>1<rt>いち</rt></ruby>

These are words that Japanese people created based on English words. Some of the most commonly used phrases are provided here, but many others exist.

アットホーム　*cozy, at-home feeling*
a tto hō mu

例　うちの<ruby>職場<rt>しょくば</rt></ruby>は、アットホームです。
Uchi no shokuba wa, atto hōmu desu.

Ex.　*Our office atmosphere is cozy.*

アラサー　*around thirty years old*

例　アラサーだから<ruby>結婚<rt>けっこん</rt></ruby>を<ruby>考<rt>かんが</rt></ruby>えないと…。

Ex.　*I'm around thirty years old...it's time to think about marriage.*

アメリカンドッグ　*corn dog*
a me ri ka n do ggu

インロック　*lock one's keys inside (a car)*
i n ro kku

イメチェン　*change one's appearance*
i me che n

例　イメチェンしたい。
Imechen shitai.

Ex.　*I want to change my appearance.*

オープンカー　*convertible*
ō pu n kā

オーダーメイド　*custom(-made)*
ō dā me i do

カンニング　*cheating (on a test)*
ka n ni n gu

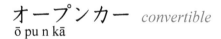

ガードマン　*security guard*
gā do ma n

キーホルダー　*key chain*
kī ho ru dā

キャッチボール *playing catch (with a ball)*
kya tchi bō ru

例 友達とキャッチボールする。
Tomodachi to kyatchi bōru suru.

Ex. *I'm going to play catch with my friend.*

例 田中さんは、会話のキャッチボールができない。
Tanaka-san wa, kaiwa no kyatchi bōru ga dekinai.

Ex. *Mr. Tanaka is not good at keeping a conversation going.*

クレーム *complaint*
ku rē mu

例 店で品物にクレームをつけた。
Mise de shinamono ni kurēmu o tsuketa.

Ex. *I complained about an item at the store.*

クラクション *car horn*
ku ra ku sho n

例 車のクラクションがうるさい。
Kuruma no kurakushon ga urusai.

Ex. *The car horn is loud.*

コンセント *electrical outlet/socket*
ko n se n to

コストダウン *reduce costs*
ko su to da u n

例 うちの会社はコストダウンが必要ですね。
Uchi no kaisha wa kosutodaun ga hitsuyō desu ne.

Ex. *Our company needs to reduce costs.*

コピーバンド *cover band*
ko pī ba n do

サラリーマン *salaried employee*
sa ra rī ma n

セロテープ *cellophane tape*
se ro tē pu

シール *sticker*
shī ru

スマート *slim*
su mā to

例 やせてスマートになった！
Yasete sumāto ni natta!

Ex. *I lost some weight and look slimmer now.*

Wasei-Eigo 2　和製英語 2
<ruby>和<rt>わ</rt>製<rt>せい</rt>英<rt>えい</rt>語<rt>ご</rt></ruby> <ruby>2<rt>に</rt></ruby>

Here are some more *wasei-eigo* terms. An English native might hesitate to use them since they sound so strange, but doing so will make your speech sound very natural to a native Japanese speaker.

タレント　*T.V. personality*
ta re n to

チャームポイント　*one's attractive qualities*
chā mu po i n to

例　君のチャームポイントは目だね。
Kimi no chāmupointo wa me da ne.

Ex.　*Your eyes are most attractive quality.*

ドンマイ　*don't worry (said for encouragement)*
do n ma i

Don't mind!
ドンマイ

例　A：あ〜あ　テストだめだった〜。
A ：　Ā~ tesuto dame datta~.

B：ドンマイ　ドンマイ、次があるよ。
B ：　Donmai donmai, tsugi ga aru yo.

Ex.　*Oh no... I failed my test.*

Don't worry about it. Tomorrow is another day.

ナイーブ　*sensitive*　　　バイキング　*buffet*
na ī bu　　　　　　　　　　ba i ki n gu

ハイテンション　*excited*
ha i te n sho n

例　今日はハイテンションだね。
Kyō wa haitenshon da ne.

Ex.　*You seem excited today.*

ハンドルキーパー　*designated driver*
ha n do ru kī pā

フリーダイヤル　*toll-free*　　　フリーサイズ　*one size fits all*
fu rī da i ya ru　　　　　　　　　fu rī sa i zu

ファイト　*Go for it!*
fa i to

例　がんばっていこう！ファイト！
Ganbatte ikou! faito!

Ex.　*Let's give 'em our best! Go!*

ヘビロテ *heavy rotation (such as a song on a radio station)*
he bi ro te

ペットボトル *plastic bottle*
pe tto bo to ru

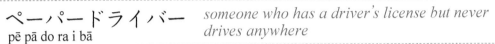

ペアルック *matching outfits*
pe a ru kku

ペーパードライバー *someone who has a driver's license but never drives anywhere*
pē pā do ra i bā

ベッドタウン *commuter town*
be ddo ta u n

ホッチキス *stapler*
ho tchi ki su

マイバッグ *one's own shopping bag*
ma i ba ggu

マイペース *at one's own pace / not easily influenced*
ma i pē su

例 田中さんはマイペースですね。
Tanaka-san wa maipēsu desu ne.

Ex. *Mr. Tanaka is always in his own little world.*

マイホーム *self-owned home (not rented)*
ma i hō mu

マンツーマン *one-on-one (lesson)*
ma n tsū ma n

例 レッスンをマンツーマンで受ける。
Ressun o mantsūman de ukeru.

Ex. *I take one-on-one lessons.*

ラブラブ *very affectionate or romantic*
ra bu ra bu

例 あの夫婦はいつもラブラブだね。
Ano fūfu wa itsumo raburabu da ne.

Ex. *That married couple is always very affectionate.*

ユーフォー *U.F.O.*
yū fō

ワンパターン *monotonous*
wa n pa tān

例 仕事が毎日ワンパターンでつまらない。
Shigoto ga mainichi wanpatān de tsumaranai.

Ex. *My day-to-day work is monotonous and boring.*

Lesson 32

Other Terms　その他<ruby>他<rt>た</rt></ruby>

Although kanji do exist for some of these words, they are often written in katakana for a variety of reasons; their kanji might be difficult, for instance, or the writer just wanted to make use of katakana's visual appeal.

Words have difficult kanji

オレ　*I (casual expression used by men)*
o re

ヒザ　*knee*
hi za

ワキ　*armpit*
wa ki

ケガ　*injury*
ke ga

バラ　*rose*
ba ra

カビ　*mold*
ka bi

Slang

マジ？　*Are you serious?*
ma ji

ネタバレ　*spoiler*
ne ta ba re

ヤバイ　*dangerous*
ya ba i

モヤモヤ　*fuzzy / feel gloomy*
mo ya mo ya

Animals / Plants

ブタ　*pig*
bu ta

アサガオ　*morning glory*
a sa ga o

ヤギ　*goat*
ya gi

ヒマワリ　*sunflower*
hi ma wa ri

Visual effects

1. To lessen a word's impact

ジャマ　*disturb*
ja ma

ワガママ　*selfish*
wa ga ma ma

ダメ　*not allowed*
da me

ケンカ　*fight / quarrel*
ke n ka

2. To make a word look cooler

オシャレ *fashionable*
o sha re

カッコイイ *cool*
ka kko i i

3. To express a sound

ドーン *low thump or boom*
dō n

トントン *knocking or drumming sound*
to n to n

ザーザー *sound of heavy rainfall*
zā zā

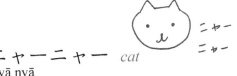

ゴシゴシ *scrubbing sound*
go shi go shi

4. To express an animal sound

ワンワン *dog*
wa n wa n

ニャーニャー *cat*
nyā nyā

ブーブー *pig*
bū bū

モー *cow*
mō

5. To express a scream

キャー *(woman)*
kyā

ワー *(man)*
wā

ウォー *(monster)*
wō

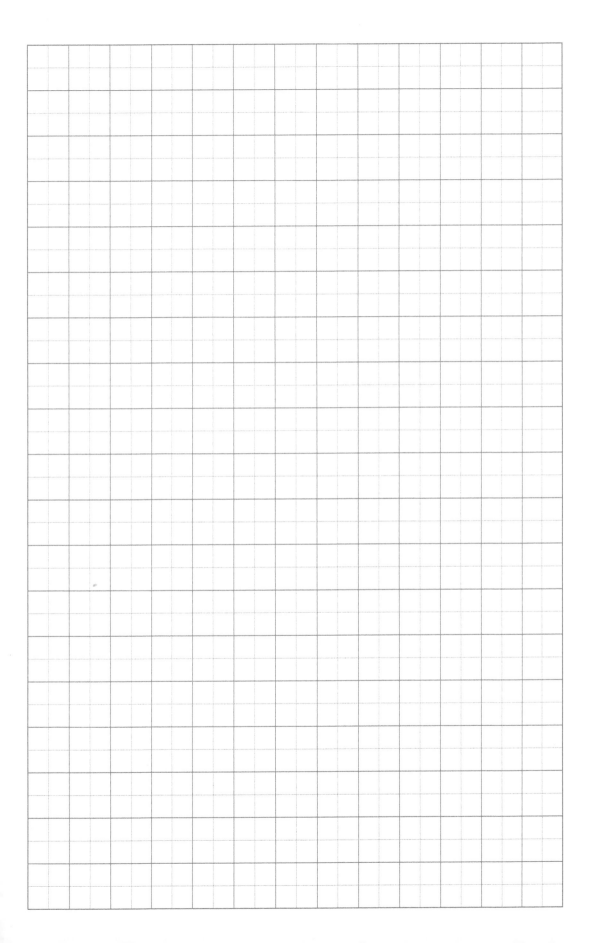

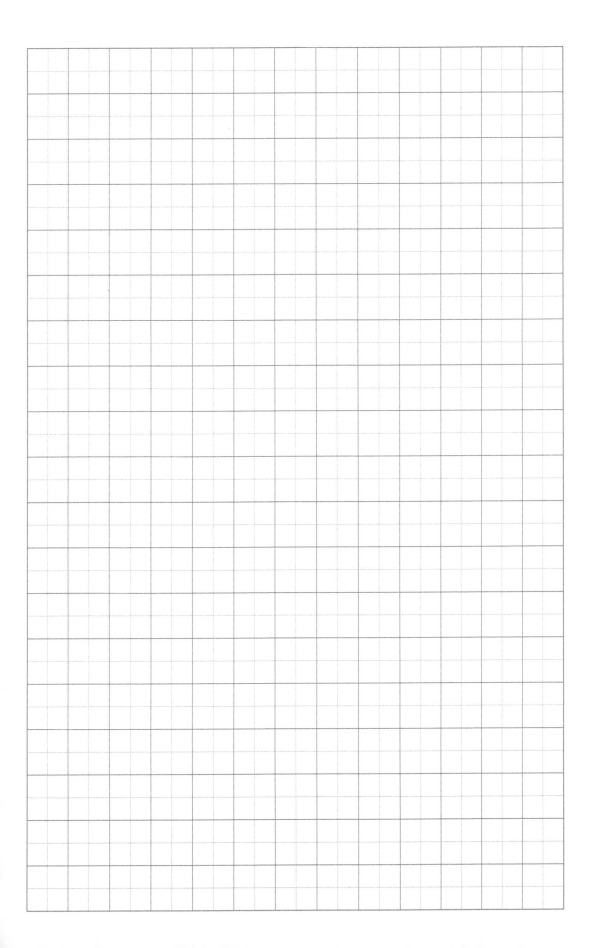

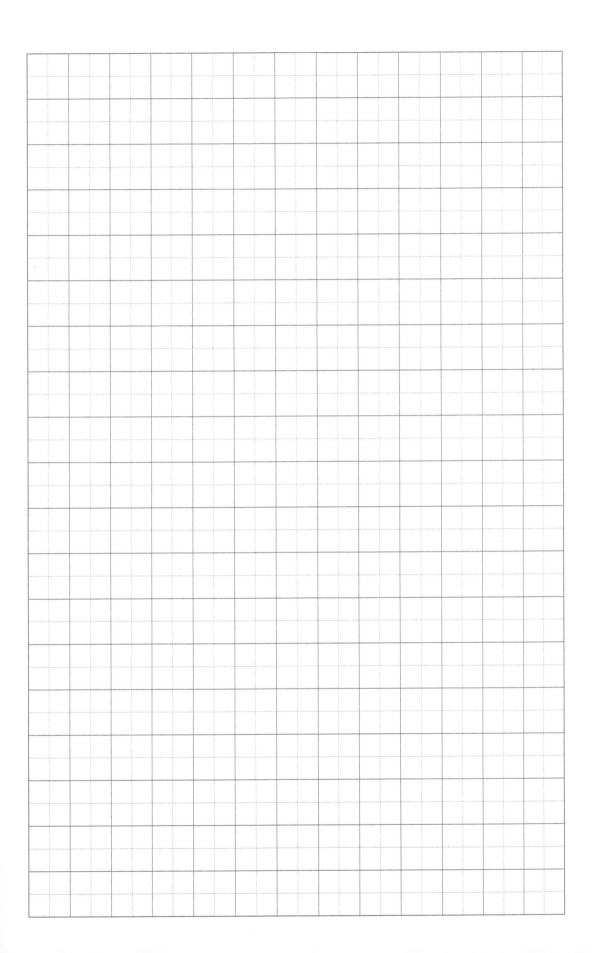

EASY AND FUN
KATAKANA

Published by
Stone Bridge Press
P. O. Box 8208, Berkeley, CA 94707 USA
sbp@stonebridge.com • www.stonebridge.com

Cover design by Linda Ronan.

Originally published in Japan in 2017 as *Easy and Fun Katakana* by IBC Publishing, Tokyo, Japan. Material used by permission.

First Stone Bridge Press international edition, 2018.

Printed in the United States of America.

10 9 8 7 6 5 4 3 2 1   2022 2021 2020 2019 2018